Joel Lewis
Vertical's Currency
New and Selected Poems

by Joel Lewis

Tossed as It Is Untroubled
Japan in a Dishpan
Bullets in the Potato Salad
Anxiety of Influence (with Michael Reardon)
Three Works
Entropia
House Rent Boogie
Palookas of the Ozone
North Jersey Gutter Helmet

Edited:
Bluestones & Salt Hay: An Anthology of New Jersey Poets
On the Level Everday: Selected Talks of Ted Berrigan
Reality Prime: Selected Poems of Walter Lowenfels

Joel Lewis

Vertical's Currency

new and selected poems

Talisman House, Publishers
Jersey City, New Jersey

Published in the United States of America by
Talisman House, Publishers
P.O. Box 3157
Jersey City, New Jersey 07303-3157

Manufactured in the United Sates of America
Printed on acid-free paper

Acknowledgments:

Some of these poems first appeared in *Angel Exhaust, First Intensity, Gare du Nord, Giants Play Well in the Drizzle, Hanging Loose, Jacket, Lingo, Long News at the Short Century, Moment's Notice* (Coffee House Press, 1993), *Newark Review, North Jersey Gutter Helmet* (Oasis Press, 1997), *New American Writing, Social Text, Talisman, Toe To Boot, The World.* Apologies for appearances forgotten due to my bad bookkeeping. Thanks to all editors.

Entropia appeared in a VERY limited edition from Gaede's Pond Press in 1986.

A notary sojac & a tip o' the hat to: Sandy, my family, Wesley Brown, Jordan Davis, Pat Ethridge, Callin Harrison, Bob Holman, Mickey Jenkins, Glen Kenny, Rochelle Kraut, Gary Lenhart, Kevin O'Reilly, Elinor Nauen, Terry Ripmaster, Bob Rosenthal, David Shapiro, Ed Smith, Chris Stroffolino, & David Trinidad for friendship, encouragement, and support along the hardscrabble shunpikes of poetry.

A brass figurine with bronze decor to: Ed Foster — not just for his support of this book (and my previous Talisman projects) — but for his yeoman work in the saltmines of the publishing planet and for being a mensch.

Library of Congress Cataloging-in-Publication Data

Lewis, Joel.
    Vertical's currency : new and selected poems / Joel Lewis
        p.   cm.
    ISBN 1-883689-84-8 (cloth : alk. paper). — ISBN 1-883689-83-x (pbk. : alk. paper)
        I. Title.
    PS3562.E9477V47   1999
    811'.54—dc21   99-18964
                                                                  CIP

"I am you."
  —Linda Tripp

"Heap see, but mighty few know."
  —Othur Turner

"Any door is a good door."
  —Ted Berrigan

CONTENTS

NERVOUS FABRIC — 91

Selected Poems

for Alice Notley
and
Maureen Owen

Shine On Brightly

Jump ship
at the first
opportunity.

You'll be glad
you did
just that.

A big whirlpool
was up ahead.

Nobody could see it
except you
& premonition.

Now you are ashore,
eating jelly donuts
& wearing the silly grin
of the dumb & temporary hero.

They want your life story,
but you know better
than that.

Tonto's Expanding Headband

What rooms lifted up and what pure
maintenance keeps the engines of North Bergen
rising? Manhattan is a cracked curtain
& its breath-rubbed pylons are fixed into
bedrock. The people I passed were whistling between
random scowls and, at the lake, a flap
of lightning flamed on a jogger.

I was only the same town from day to day
& was soon among the radios of my failures
inside the pizzeria. And I *heard* my
fortune cookie fate announced in that cell
of brutal money. And this is what
I write out of: a walking life.

Blue Comedy

"Yours is not to complete
the work, **but neither are you
free to abstain from it** ."
—Rabbi Tarphon, *Pirkei Avot* (2:21)

Paterson's fountains fade as this bus
soldiers into slow departure. Broad Street:
the linking reed between Silk City and Newark
& watch bluestone curbs give way to the politics
of manicured lawns, neat neck-tied men
& dreamy Portugese chewing cotton candy
on flagstone stoops.

Against the Legal-Anglo world,
absent coins manage a jangling
sound. And all I hear on my Walkman
is rain and sparks. And my brain —
hard, enlarged and crisp as an iceberg lettuce —
reads this world as a rapid forest.

The Passaic's jade-colored water
squeezes past the Lackawanna trestle
and steaming paella is another name for lava
in the Ironbound.

Puddles of Wisdom[*]

Fuji Blimp over Hoboken
    still in the same chunk of sky
I left it when boarding the Dover local
    to see the Dali Lama
at the Newark Museum. I was inattentively
    fortunate to meet Martin R.,
Fort Manno & Kate C. — now renamed "Arizona"
    & **not** after Mark Lindsay's dreck-of-ages song.
"It came in a vision," Kate tells me, & why not?
    I see prayer flags over Brood Street
and the stewing Passaic is merely a named
    object in the sentient world. I walk
on Newark's gilded and splintered streets
    to a world where nothing gets invented,
accepting the terms of a policy
    of kindness; afterwards, vino verde
in the Ironbound, near the stelle
    that's Davey Tough's headprint.

---

[*]"No room for squares" Dept.: Davey Tough, great drummer of the swing/bop transitional period, was killed when he fell and his head hit a Newark curb, 1949.

Winter Evening, Passaic

My brain eats
dust and this city
gained its name from
the Lenni Lenape phrase
for "valley," though
in these sub-
charming surroundings
I only hear the liquid melody
of scavengers coming
from your vest.

The beginning layers of rain
age the river view. Prepare
the table. Streetlamps
splintering into each other.

Hoboken Early Sunday Morning

In the middle
of the Jersey Junction viaduct
I saw an old man wearing a baseball cap backwards,
like a Rutgers frat brother.

He was walking the early morning darkness
to Schaefer's Diner on 14th Street.
He had a jaunty, old time stride
like he owned the empty, sleeping city
in his head.

Joel Lewis

when we go

for Bill Frissell

60 mph: gusts up Washington Street like Velcro
for the advanced. Tough button
Hathaway shirt won't help
— home clumps in the Heights gone black.
A thousand brisk skies in store windows.

How to rewrite the demands of solar influence?
Chattering in loanwords, the spongeware bowl clasps
a braid of lightning. In sly belief of cradling peripheries
shy children make arithmetic of the streets, nonstop
towards an awning. Little umbrellas. The river, no stars.

Market Street, Newark

The lightning time is long past
and the joke is on those who have
least to laugh about. Market & Broad —
the heart of this fading gridwork
with my moment here, to enter
the Federal Courthouse in parody
of the respectable American going somewhere
with purpose. These avenues are incredible.
A touch of brimstone from dioxin-tainted
Ironbound inflates the tonsils
and beneath an anger that's in these passing faces
are people closer to me than I'd like
to think. Somewhere, stacks of banknotes
wait to be counted & someplace further west
the Malls lure the dislocated
towards tiled Niagaras.

Nothing sadder than a department store haunted
by its age, some bad alchemy has
affected its golden engines
and the astrology of human hunger
is today's ragged line at a soup kitchen
behind the statues in Military Park.

A boom-box breaks the abstract review with hip-hop
marching orders, edicts delivered
to the eloquence that's people walking
to nowhere in common. They all muster silence in what is
left past the collapse of the dollar's
totem and if I cried out, who would hear me
on this annex of American homegrown Third World?
Everything blends with the dominant reality
that's in the national bloodstream
and its daily performance darkens the landscape
and what of appetite except that it's named
desire, everywhere and in everyone

Joel Lewis

on this dismantled scenery,
the wind playing sunset checkers
with clouds of Big Mac wrappers.

Route 3, Nutley (*Mad*)

Here, near the valium fulcrum, the noise car stalls, with red
repeaters dashed into the gum-ball darkness. Looming on the
shirtside of this highway are the flapjack eaters & their godson:
& on this remission barrier, one nonstop voice
makes me long for the stammering vocals
& irregular phrasings of Grand Funk Railroad.

Landmarked against the monopoly of space,
the girl repeater hums cracked Madlibs into
the Jersey darkness. I'm unhooking.
The momentum of the maps proceeds toll barriers,
covers the bets on the gods & the guardians of noise.
My captivity underwritten by acoustic leaks.

At the Shrine of Lou Costello, Paterson*

There's a lot I want to say
in this voice, but nothing seems
to fit. Some shakiness
on the curbs & I'll use this
downtime to seal up this sack of crullers
& board this Paterson-bound bus that

traces the old college route
& back then, as now: brainless
as a biscuit with the same strange
daydream of Gramsci playing drums
with Ornette Coleman. So I'm not

a pilgrim, I just play one on TV
& I have some stupid human estrangement
in this city, but I hope I won't run into him
& the buildings seem colored in
by magic markers. Nothing to say really,
but saying it. At the Great Falls

I stand alone with my language, the chlorine
sting stands in advance of the real night.

---

*Non-irony symbolism department: There really is a Lou Costello statue in
Paterson, located on Cianci Street, a few blocks from downtown's Main Street. Costello is
posed holding a baseball bat, a reference to the classic Abbot & Costello "Who's on first?"
routine.

Bergenline Avenue, Union City

Do I smell homecooking?

No. It's only the Hudson River
nourished by Sandy Hook red tide.
That brackish estuary is the Greenwich Observatory
for Union City, where noise cars
surface from sub-silt furrows
to the money that's salted inside the hollows
of the Watchung Mountains.

Next to the calla lilies
of the War Zone Florists
I sip on what's left inside
a styro of café con leché while
thinking of the Kwakiutl Indians
and their "Dance of Giving Away Property"
— their Big Winner a sure social failure
in this immigrant hardscrabble dreamsville.

Minus Water

If you knew more about the future, the past
would be even more difficult. Night wakes us
to details of the road. Cars cool
in the Kinney lot, the strapped ferry is moored
like a solid mechanical friend.
What is the quizzical steam moneying
from the white wedge of the Citicorp Center?
It's an iodine lamp. It's nowhere at dusk.
It's all a shuffling summed up in the winds above the city.
Jersey is out of work, traffic lights emerge
as my rooms. The moving house of the Palisades
is a nominative force — I'm nearly golden,
& there's this long street ahead of me tonight.

Been Here, Done That

for Kevin O'Reilly

The old neighborhood is imbedded
with our actions, though the harm
that lived through the streets
managed to ignore us. We were always
hatless in the grey, polished air
& we took our best cues
from the boomerang vector
of Betty Brite Cleaners.

In the magazine version of an aromatic
sunset we walked the curbs
of Kennedy Boulevard expecting nothing
less than normality and a Yoo-Hoo
from **Mezzy's**. Sleet against
safety glass, we travelled roads
where things whip towards the center.

Angels did not rise from the Hackensack Meadows
to amuse us and, in another poem, a once
young man thinks about the power of destiny
in a rare pleasant mood. And I know that
I've been here before. And that we do inhabit this House,
in this poem at least, our senses attentive
to the assurance of a plenitude.

Joel Lewis

Fringe Parking

Wake-up as an outcast of Passaic.
Trees in duplicity.
My eyelids worn raw.

Wake up as paranormal.
Shift weight to the feet.
Crease the hands
so the pen stays in place.

I was born with the radio on.

Dear Kevin: grow out from
under your Dunkirk.
Suggested diagnosis
— Another Green World.

A dark side to forecast.
Freed of fine lines   Wake-up
against details of constraint.

Dear Sally: why did your family
dog want to separate the meat
from my bones?

Raw eyelids shift the weight
to shaking fingers.

Intensified enforced traffic.
Growth stays placed.
Rain hanging:
an American style.

Dear Nancy: beautiful common things.

Thought buffalos inactive
Woke focused.   Flashes of other echoes.

Symptom: pedestrian idealism.
Dear Maureen: Woke-up
emulating the Big Mistake.

Rule 1-a: All we ask the reader for is domination.

There's a revival
of Norbert Weiner in certain places.
Duplex trees.   Common beautiful things.

A fucking ocean.
Details of meat.
Knees: another luxury.
The family dog with tiny antelope ears.

Woke-up   Discovered I was
a Juke Box with salami.

A theoretical Smokey The Bear.
Deformed rabbis spin joyless propellers
nailed to their yarmulkes.

Hopeless chronicle of an imaginary town.
Not attached to misprints in my bible.

Dear Ted: There's a poem behind
his immensity of space.
Rain hanging over ersatz Rome.
A lodge, that's all: Burundi's ladder.

In Paterson — 1

Train sets off to
the gap formed
by Goffle Brook,
and that leaves me
on the Market Street trestle
as the mirror of empty
municipal politics. I repocket
a Chicken McNugget, then
breathe to taste
the local soup called "air."
Now refreshed, I think:

> *Why do the remaining*
> *white men of Paterson look*
> *like Orville Redenbacher?*

I pass the restaurant
of the blue moon matchbooks,
where the moody people of Dalmatia
eat their native dish
of wire spaghetti, washed down
by bottles of black cherry soda

The self in a welter of Others.
A city as series of false alarms.
Peddlers on Market Street
hawk poloroid prints
of Garret Mountain's
marine intrusion.

In Paterson — 2

Locked drab and sudden,
Paterson as a thin flower force.

Winter pavements
take the shoeprints
of eighty languages.

Humming oil
jangling in these
gummy nerves. Malcolm,

hand me that ragged
Delawanna schedule.

I stand
unseen.

In Paterson — 3

Streets wide enough to welcome soot.
Honey-colored lots. A black man
with lumbago. Car radio: **Traffic's** "Dear Mr. Fantasy"
— **Why?** A Circassian family walks Ellison Street
as if they just crossed a cantilever bridge.
I hear two bus drivers speak a smooth
& idiomatic Pig Latin. Streetlamps
go on, revealing a urine pucks,
cappucinno spoons and lottery tickets. A goat
is eating my manuscripts.

Lou Costello, 1942 (In Paterson — 4)

"Hello out there to all
the people there
in Paterson" is how Lou Costello
ended his radio show.

And in the jumbo shrimp neighborhoods
of Paterson, where archeologists
huddled together in squatter dorms,
women lifted their heads
from the Old Gold haze of canasta
& liverwurst parties to shout
"**That's** our Lou!" — then back
to the business at hand.

In their minds, Lou is sleeping
on the leather lobby couch
of the Alexander Hamilton Hotel.
Family troubles. Moonlight is coating
the floor & the tuba-faced night clerk
gets his blubbery fingertips dirty
scanning the want ads
of a "nite owl"
Paterson Morning call.

Joel Lewis

In the Great Falls Historic District (In Paterson — 5)

In 1976,
Gerald Ford came
to dedicate the Great Falls,
wave to elderly Republicans
& eat shrimp toast
at the House of Shih
— fondly called House of **Shit**
by unnerved residents
who know all too well
that there ain't no Santa Claus
on the evening stage
& that the tab keeps
getting run up
& that nobody here wants to get paid
to be the boss.

It's summer somewhere
in the Western Hemisphere.
Twenty-two proud Latino flags
hang in the Paterson Cathedral.
I hear Paterson's common cry:
"Where's my paycheck, **you bastard!**"

This city
could probably use your ideas.

In Paterson — 6

Heaven is deep in the scales
of a Cianci Street Salumena. Burly
men leave thumbprints
in the styros of espresso
they've been nursing all morning.
And in their dreams, they dream of keno

& I, non-observer to these events, get
restless when the immobile
suddeness of winter hits. A little brio
for the indigent. Dogs, probably terriers,
direct their barks towards
AFM Local 18's terra-cotta &
gingerbread HQ. My speech
at the lockpicker's luncheon failed miserably.

Bluntboats all night. I hear them
surging on the Passaic,
groaning with traprock.
The wind strikes solid
on their rusty sides.

This is no place to wait out
time, though the air tonight
smells like Velamints
& the Watchung sunset reminds me
of tomato paste.

In Paterson — 7

Now another finality — back streets
like unlit windows, cappucinno
hour-by-hour, that chilling sleep
of orphans.

And the people passing the
Broadway Bus Terminal
resemble the ancients of Phoenecia
In matter of height and diet

& the city **is** a series
of false alarms & the law of exchange
gets reinvented when another
Libby's chili dog is bartered
for chump change.

The Passiac smells like malt Ovaltine.
Waitresses sing Circassian boat songs into
the sleeping ears of a nighthawk. Lewis
tells me: "Joel, I know just how you feel about
Paterson. Every night, I dream about
The Bronx in color."

Gravity Fails

Neat neck-tie civilization
against the abrupt clarity
of dinner conversations.

In those days everything
was strange.

B&W video of the Jimi Hendrix Experience
"Wind Cries Mary" & so hard to spot
a lip sync in progress.

Have you bought any biodegradeables lately?

Squirrels are afraid of
sweet corn.

Seeing little, I depend
on my ears for the bad news.

◨ ◨ ◨

Let's call improvising musicians
"tone scientists" from now on.

Captain Piddingron
coined the word
"cyclone" in 1844.

A beer commercial's version of Africa.

Consciousness is not only memory
but admonition.

The question of details:
ribbed rim of a dime in a
chump-change of pennies.

Sound can wash clothes.

All spider songs are instrumental.

◙ ◙ ◙

When does twilight end?Answer: when
the sun is 18 degrees
below the horizon.

The mechanical planet
where grief is pneumatic.

Early New World Settlers debated
whether the Hummingbird was really
a "bird" or a "West Indian bee."

She flips him the
paper cup salute.

The day after "tornado patterns" showed up in a
scientists's jar of bear grease eight "twisters"
crashed into the Midwest.

◙ ◙ ◙

In Singapore, there is always a ship on the horizon.

Lunar soil has no organic content.

I invent lovely names for the strangers.

◙ ◙ ◙

Arab names left little imprint on popular astronomy
but those lights still people the hungry sea.

Newark 1812: "Gardens & Fields covered with snow at noon."

By 1908, he announced that he had
found the most sensitive weather
plants from all over the world.

I can trace the progress of a gust
moving down the length of the
lowlands.

◙ ◙ ◙

Raised to be agreeable.

The bean is a strange vegetable.

Necco wafer: an uncommon resident.

◙ ◙ ◙

Pinpoint localities.

Junkyard for the ancient texts.

The moon always shows the same face to the Earth.

He was judged in a solid dialect.

◙ ◙ ◙

Joel Lewis

For the purpose of clarity
they cut out his tongue.

◧ ◧ ◧

A day of invention: "Take this tape back
to your Scotch bosses & tell 'em to put
some glue on it!"

◧ ◧ ◧

The glow of insomnia upon glass.

Moonlight on the telephone in the small window.

I explained the monetary answer.

◧ ◧ ◧

There were no sunspots during the years 1645 to 1715.

Humor is the very essence of a democratic society.

You have to believe in the gods to see them.

I don't trust warm and friendly people.

◧ ◧ ◧

A language landlocked in equally authoritative texts. None of these insects have
electrical spasms. There is nothing you can do with a really dedicated misfit. I
could rule the world if I could only get the parts. He was born to laugh at torna-
does. A pointed account of People-You-Know. Give me convenience or give me
death.

◧ ◧ ◧

World of frost and ice made
innocent. Call it: The Little Ice Age.
    Paired white & Black mules: a Jersey Team.
    Apple Jack is Jersey Lightning.
    14 donuts: a Jersey Dozen.
Latin was a required course in barber colleges. The record of past floods can be
found in the slackwater. Bees and wasps puncture ripe fruits, too. The Japanese
girl stands quiet there.

Up in Lakeville

Modernity is not of much interest here.
In the morning, the lynx
scours Millerton Road looking
to make breakfast out of a family cat
left to its devices. And at night,
Johnny Mathis' loyalist fan in Salisbury
weeps alone as he listens to
"I could have kept on dancing"
on his 8-track player.

I am here with my skin
for once. The twins are here too,
dressed akimbo. The beautiful young
poet's texts are so condensed she
writes them on the back
of Bazooka Joe comics.

The man from Grand Island admires
the aluminum jewels of his father's
fountain pen. "Go home
& make yourself a sandwich,"
says a voice from somewhere there.

Everyone here with borrowed warmth.
Woman with a greasy heart, her
automatic man. Tanzanian peaberry
caffeinating my system like pine tar
mental grip. And it's all so easy to see.
She leaves me with this small room.

North Jersey Gutter Helmet

as expanding as
cucumber slumber
or call it a rotary a
roundabout a traffic circle

memory of the Autobahn
Hitler not Kraftwerk
decant on Bendix's Teterboro
cicadas buzz like a bad-reed Shorter
or call it "the politics of rachmones"

each clearing of the brain
brings a further clearing
of the brain as in braindeer,
Braintree, Brainiac, brains beneath
the floorboard, call it Signac

or don't call it Signac
Bayonne = Oil City
mustard goes on the wiener silently
bring it up, slow dazzle
dinner is getting cold

a syntax that strains sound
don't call them Guidos!
new pencil on patrol
the grateful ones at the traffic light
So why does it articulate?

Boxtops' followup to "The Letter": a flop
buzzy from that sixth cup of Vienna Roast
no merit along Kinderkamack Road
lethal housefrau, that one
a sudden Totowa (or **else**)

Joel Lewis

Karmablast of Yoo-Hoo or insane
Fizzies from memory better used on
visualizing whirled peas
Fathom that? Now the rude craze . . .
& here it is: Goffle Brook Road, plain.

So Vinnie's backyard was the dirty, dirty Passaic
No duty to share this save
A conflation of factoids.
Savor old Stones' B-side "I'm Free."
Ink dictating itself.

I'm investing in these old hands
"Asshole!" shouted, 1:00 am, Hoboken
we're not on an island
Did I tell you about internal colonialization?
waiting for your smoke signal

this my table today
a succession of cuddly gum chewers
farting in a museum
remnants of the Morris Canal
a Circassian rage: car stall on Kamena street

some truculent zeds
OK, I'm doing the best
I can not enough nothing
pops up in the mind Pop
Tarts: quiescent American snack

streets I walked on: Passaic
risk of severe emotional disturbance
if I could get *that* sound
Moving water: Berry's Creek
I write that one there

North Jersey Gutter Greeting: **"What are**
you **looking** *at,* **ASSFACE!"**
A sausage is chasing, me down the street
Our nation of no pain
The brain of "doubt crossed my mind."

A place in Hackensack: The Transfer Station
Just *smell* that hot bean pie, many
connective gestures just
pass me that Talmud, Bwana
seems a case of Quink geometry

got my totem working
where Chief Oratam had his crib
this is a good old day
Ed Sullivan trampoline memories
She wrote me a letter of thanks.

Imagine correcting pronouns for a living, scary
my no-hat is littered with Hebrew letters
or a house with bad windows bad
omens, Baden-Baden, my name
is ringing, bad medicine, bad hand-live

back-to-back corporate manual readers.
I remember Corduroy Village, a store not a town
ULP!, pelican daughters & their
kin, thank you distractors
thank you boat shoes

three variations of interference
Snake Hill remade nice renamed Laurel Hill
slightly all the time
& you, Ace, learn to see what others
thought they've seen

so, articulate again, thoughts to go
where are *you*, Mott the Hoople?
frame a texture with a lesser form of salsa
Mahawah that slab of Ho-Ho- Kus
You, bleeding gums, **WAKE UP!**

Stab the connectives you
who look so like me
a firm model of social paranoia
Jersey skeeter, complete with saddle
there is no superiority.

Househunting in Hoboken: obligatory
Huey Lewis CD in every condo.
Got a case of nerve nets
man, who can stand it? Say, Fidel,
rent me a raft or an aged cigar

Count it off with Larry Graham's thumb
or a band called Shlomo & His Mendicants
Through the loose rain, I see Moonachie
Vapors & a bowl of salt.
Patience, not enlightenment.

This Old School personalism, moneygrip
toney edges plague the drive to closure.
I believe in the true polar front.
Small room filled with gravity
& you must pay & the price is lucid

Air guitar variations, the guttersnipe
up in Garret Mountain, "I regret
nothing" — who said that, Piaf or Fidel?
Don't call me Nature Boy!
The talk is slow in Rockleigh.

Numbers in time of trouble
that Steinway seems to have
rabies, some calm rustic
synthesis, my name is ringing, ye fiends, ye
cold gendarmes of avante-garde poetry!

That pile of shit the mass culture calls
GOD, and a tincture of the good stuff
& maybe you'd rather be in Jersey City
having beautiful thoughts. Bad medicine. No
end to things built of human talk.

Making a Meal out of It

Hoboken snowtime and the big slushy
mounds are the laundry of the future,
with next-door's mortician rating
my clumsy shoveling by shouting:
"You'd never make it as a gravedigger!"

Time pulse quickens with walkers
and sidewalk lackeys merged in a quadrille
of symbiosis. In the windows of the shops
they sell devices capable

of reordering speech. I pass. I have
an exile's sense of recreation
& believe some sort of rebirth possible
from the wreck of our common misery
& that songs are clear when sung

by heroes, but not in this epoch. Niggling
winter dreams fueled by the rhythms
of the world's desire. This is my version.
I know the dimensions. I live by a river.

Spinner

Think of a lavish papery conversation,
forget what the words implied just
think of the tone, the tone of the words
trying to surf above the sine waves
of dialectical static. Juke Box starts up:
Herb Alpert and His Tijuana Brass
and the "Lonely Bull" makes some
smile. My boogie men are not unionized,
but my better parts are on extended holiday.
They call this kind of house paint
"dark as a doll" and they sell it to mendicants.
The wildest dreams of wildmen
still recommend themselves.

Joel Lewis

The Piano On Canal

for Ted Berrigan

Hostility taught me nothing.
The rewards of poetry not immediate;
then never blooming in the patterns
you'd think it could.

The Great Falls unhitching from snow
is plenty excitement
for a February Paterson evening,
here where phony monolithic politics
vanished before I was equal to the syntax.

> *Main Street's Woolworth's sno-cone shaver stood*
> *silent in the slight morning air.*
> *The low industrial sounds went undetected*
> *by the gloss of surveillance & the active lives*
> *at the local diner counters conducted their*
> *routines in the spirit*
> *of narrative concealment. it seemed that friends*
> *grew fewer, further, though more dependable*
> *& it was a Colorado zephyr that honed*
> *my confidence, though that Jersey cadence*
> *made me long for the Homes that I am.*

A blue tropicana Meadowsky
and we're inside it, travelling through
this landscape in Kevin's Plymouth.
"**MOVE!** you Dog-**Bastard**," he is screaming
at a Valiant on pocked Communipaw
with we three still moving, some stalling,
navigating across this empire
of trance, one new
happy return.

One Red Rose That I Mean

Taped message from Paul: "Hey
what **was** the name of that Duke
Ellington album you told me
about?"

    Night time/early autumn/Hoboken chill
    enough to keep revelers away
    perhaps to do that keg in home comfort

& What to think/make of . . .

    that Stephen Foster penned *Beautiful Dreamer*
    in a Bloomfield Street boarding house?

Jingling monotone of urban uhuru man me
separates my two thoughts thru coffee.
The river at my back rhymes with some other poem.
Worldbeat's nervous rhythms thru speakers.
Take it all unwrapped
Glimmers of the merely "dear possible" &, so,
not to autograph *that* aside.

    I reject the punk democracy of old feelings
    & am not a receptive citizen
    or even citizenry.
    I mean
    do I look like a Norwegian to **you**, Bwana?

Joel Lewis

Dub Housing

Try this: "**Mad Jersey hurt him into prose?**"
Write this?: *"The bass lie deep, still afraid of the Indians."*
Read Columbia's **Literary History of the United States** mostly
middle-aged white guys not too gay   a little or very drunk
     My own edifice: bewildered by the presentiment of clocks.
That dream of being useful   solid   a citizen like
that inventor of the parking meter   first appearing
in Dust Bowl Depression Oklahoma City

Charles Olson, to his Brandeis audience: *"You people
are so literate that I don't want to read
to you anymore!"*   Man in raincoat, cloudless sky
     The lost tribes appear as the skeleton of a poem just as
     Paul Chambers held up a **specific segment** of America with
     his bass playing.

Try this: write this?
Dark & hideous rain drops coat our rowboat
Light's grip is accidental, the pace of slow traffic
          that I was born to laugh at tornados.

Entropia

for Bill Berkson

Sky was lumps. And jujubees of cobblestone slaked the surface. A statue: Sam Sloan, who brought the old Lackawanna rail from mere staples to a power of maps and boldness. The compass never intended this sort of progression to shortfall. Coffee swerves, it's my caffeine plasma. I took the telephone to its far extent and thought quick of 1949's last trolley, 1967's end of the ferry. see me dripping in this stuff. It must be a time for marketing. A lame land shot full of traffic cones. Blinky kind of Trivial Pursuit revisionings. World seems slender, and cracks in the tiny slant between Duke's Bar and the parking lot run by the Latvian Mob. I've had it, and just before I'm scheduled to go on. Here. *You* take it from here. No! Then let fall. Under a Kleenex dome, my cartel of turmoils slides through the carbons. Hoof it. On goes the backpack with the windmill attachments. Tongue won't divulge this river's bright kliegs. Reduction. Blamed Heat News.

"There is a divine covenant in everyone's heart:
to love his native soil — despite its climate."

—Midrash

Railroad overpass and the homeless men who live beneath. Rivers of tracks spill over the cleanfill. Bluestone walls form a floppy ghost rust label. NEW JERSEY RESTAURANT. Deeping cold, strewn stalks form empty reflecting pools. Farm a descriptive code like particles of soft closure, or stained morning with a tugboat steaming on the condom soup natives dub "Upper Bay." Breakfast: ozone hoagies. MY-T-FINE: ghost junket factory once springboard for rennet custard. The road is pits, taffytar and the regeneration of non-economic security. Skyline sizzles dim along the chicory plants. Those men live on mattresses, with a collective chest-of-drawers secured by a small, vicious dog. No neighbors and left to be dim and oblique as calendars. Coax response from the old gas pumps. I miss the word 'jalopy.' Train rumbles, scatters age-dust upon backpacks. "You live where you live & you don't have to defend it!" Slaps of our feet tend to laggard. A shattered Brunswick Stew stamped with Ipana labels. The McAllister Tugboat Yards with a Jamaican guard bemused at our backpack enthusiasm. A black finger points a trail towards the Morris Canal Basin. Sweat grows colorless. Dogs bark from unmonitored chains. Units of Rope's ownership.

"To see everything as flat."
—Gertrude Stein

Call it what the cans call it and you'd see it all better from beneath their versions
of empty shopping. The Upper Bay is torn into six versions of the same history.
Fifty years a workingman's boat club and now the State Apparatus appears to wipe
it off the Morris Canal Boat Basin, replaced with the outshoots of a money dream.
What's this dust and sadness so bright not to be given its return as Fizzies. I started
to speak halting Esperanto, everyone around me whipped out green buttons. I saw
Manhattan from a Norway rat's point of departure. And it's all harmonics anyway,
in fact it's a gas. And what's 'fun' except to underwrite the watercooler. A few
tugs pester the visual chords. Zeroes erupt in salutations. Clownish beer music
coming from somewhere there. What angles? The boat shacks are peeled-up by the
same men who bragged them into existence. Fancy goods. "The real woe of this
event passed before her sight as some sham tragedy of the stage." Love me, love
my poetry. The hike leader is boiled speechless. I run on beans. Laser beams.

"People that enjoy echoes —
they're just bumping their mothers!"
—Don Van Vleit

Water is blunders.
My sunscreen
the simple tin teardrop
lapping at the polyrhythms
of the decaying land
building itself towards
ersatz subtle esplanade
a bland realism
for the non-industrial path
that a barely Liberty State Park
is slim payoff for converting
this Pavonia (Dutch 'land of the peacocks')
into Manhattan's sleepdirt-across-the-water.

No mystery to me,
resonant winds slip
under the piers.

"Do I smell? I smell Home Cooking.
It's only the river, it's only the river."
—David Byrne

Soda at the Greeks upon a sliver called Exchange Place. Skyline looks like Indian flint swaddled in old man's underwear. We are only episodic containers of meaning. We form a MASS. We live mostly in haphazard panic beyond and above any meaning. Harry S. Truman: "Never kick a fiesh turd on a hot day." There go the sugar beets rolling along the CNJ rail sidings. What am I saying without story or reasonable viewpoint? Isaac Abravenal: "God used the principle of nature to create language and the principle of language to create man." I order ice tea and am handed the brains behind the apparatus of decay. A box turtle with the face of Joan Rivers. At left the largest soap plant in the WORLD! Dead right — a giant billboard for a single weekend for Couch Potatoes. "What does entropy mean for today's exciting singles lifestlye???" Kids move up the empty toejam street. One walker splits down the PATH train entrance with her good looks and terrible personality. I've got those turtle dreams. The mess is up ahead. The mess is up ahead. The mess is up ahead past the soap cake monument.

Joel Lewis

"You ignorant, ill-bred foreigners! If you don't like
the way I'm doing things out there, why don't you
just pack up & go back to your own countries!"
—'Chief' Bender, American Indian
baseball pitcher, to jeering fans, circa 1910

They gave me the New Jersey franchise and look what I've done with it! I don't need psychotherapy or est — I need money! Where are the deer and dachshund in Jersey City? The career of a factory that resembles a contagious hospital. Broken bottles as ghost beads by the Schiavonne-Bonomo recycling plant. Words in the grip of nothing. The unnamed is us. Roofs the shade of fruit flies. Sun treats us like Canadian slab bacon. So we all gathered Chinese box kites and named each 'Mel.' And like Teflon, we couldn't stick to any of the things we were passing over. It was all sinking into the landfill, anyhow. Clouds were soft cling peaches. We found a trestle to take us over Jello waters. The water was filled with Elvin Jones's broken drum sticks. The water framed the shore. Susquehanna. Lackawanna. B&O. Lehigh Valley. CNJ. Pennsy. Erie. Rails seem retreating under this mud ranch. My baloney sandwich had been oxidized. What I thought was soda is liquid sneakers. Flaws in capitalism make for puffy brains. Last chance to view this dull vacancy before townhouses will roll in with the Turkish Taffy tide. Where will the poor people go? They'll just go. Sky is fledgling banana shades. We see Miss Liberty swaying under the demands of money. The field stretches wider than imagined. From the crest of Harborside Terminal, I see longshoremen load a barge full with flaming donuts.

"Finally sight permits the ranom."
                —Rae Armantrout

rigid sun   glass pier
          pre-normal potion

                              Communipaw Avenue

          the odd periscope
            of the Citicorp Tower

this stumbling live over nerves

     blazes   bay tower

                              thin grass flags

drip
  so
     tense

               air batters
                 one molten stream

               solid body
                 changes mind

Joel Lewis

"The thin film of writing becomes
a movement of strata . . ."
—Michel de Certeau

The theoretical arrangements deepen. Jersey City suffers from 'Oakland (CA) Syndrome.' In Entropia, the raggy clouds have grease spots on them. In Post-Modern culture, the crows lip- synch their caws. I float above the crumbles. What is mirage but imagination? It's drab, it's you! Walking about without focusing is the closest you'll get to an objective eye. Time and history are not made of turds. The traditional solution to problems of epistemological doubt: a nice, hot bath. As useful as watching other people sleep. Flat cluster of some unnamed, raised failspot. Monkey farts are a documented fact. I discover a ripe tomato patch growing among the empty wine bottles of Caven Point. Everyone who dreams in color — raise your hands. Spitts of weeds seem to shake towards the empty hulls of once-factories. Club Med for Seagulls.

"You've got to find some way of
saying it without saying it."
                    —Duke Ellington

          quartz birds   choice corners
              water shifts its gains

New music: Azimuth

              Tugboat: Crayfish green

     firm irritations
                              & makes it move.

          □□□□□□□□□□

          Birds   & their pajamas
                              ((Ragweed Acres

     glass pier

     tuna air

              steamed hatch   wisps

 bubbling inlet
 (bubbling inlet)

"I spread myself around: my whole little
universe in crumbs; at the center; what?"
—Roland Barthes

Late afternoon sounds splatter on this flask of green grass mixed with stone. Water
is a kind of masonry. Entropia is money's future. Water the shade of Steak-Umms.
Real Estate is an enigmatic composer straining towards an ugly music of the
future. After listening to her political views I think: ". . . is stupidity the absence of
knowledge or the acquisition of wrong knowledge?" Capitalism will crowd you
out of your life. Clear memory of a different poem. On the scrub-brush opposite
Liberty Island will rise Port Liberté, wrapped in the desperate dreams of Yuppipo-
tamia. Error is something poetry can tolerate. Rubble radiates up from the rubble.
No use in trying to clarify the text of the world. In almost every poem, one line
will refer back to the construction of the whole. Trust all these gestures. Staten
Island a southward detail that dresses the Lower Bay. The enigma of the consumer
sphinx. I subscribe to the round-earth theory.

"In idleness I am of no thickness,
I am the thinnest wafer."
—Henry D. Thoreau

Call Caven Point a decay and the steam of Upper Bay a hairy lather. It's all pouring down about my bobsled and soldered to the tune of America's indigenous plastic fictions. On another coast, the immigrant's son is cheapening our speech. He's followed by the Black preacher and this gets rowed into my head by the yeomen. I need a beautician for my brain. And if you won't want to go on, you'll still be forced along for the ride. The dirt on Henderson Street looks like breakfast flakes. Along the Morris Canal Boat Basin it seemed to be fried onyx marbles. Above: the ziggurat of the Jersey City Medical Center. Partial knowledge is the *normal* condition of living in the context of words. And David Clayton-Thomas is singing the praises of *Zest* soap cakes. The circulation of language as poetry is strikingly similar to the circulation of money as capital — poetry as the *surplus value* of language? Sunken wrecks on the maps, but too far from the eyes. I'm at the old/restored CNJ ferry terminal watching square dancers do a hot Virginia Reel. A radio station that only plays love songs: what a wretched idea! Good enough to fold sheets.

Joel Lewis

"Intense lights, vague shadows, great pillars in a
horizon are difficult things to nail signboards to."
—Charles Ives

Played (burnt) out and trailing the coded Bayonne sun on this strange Burma Road
which really is the name of it. Words are the back-doors out from solitary diner
talks. Another palace of gelt rising in the World Trade Center complex. The great
figure of a liberated civilization would be the amateur. The further it gets, 'the
writing' takes on a significance greater than its place among Things. 'Engrossed
in Art' is one way to skirt the legal trade. I'm reading 'knock-knock' jokes off the
leaking barrels of PCB's. And here is what we came for: disarmed Miss Liberty in
a humungous peach crate external girdle. New Colossus protrudes like a Milkbone
over the clutter of Entropia, and believe myself a radio to the ingratiating feelings
of dull patriotic scrimshaw. It all looks like 'dull adjectives.' The waterfront is
grouted by a cookie cutter. It is therefore in the abyss of the proper that we are
going to try to recognize the impossible idiom of a signature. Thus relatively few
outsiders are familiar with the surface of this city, spread upon a peninsula be-
tween the Hudson and Hackensack Rivers, directly west of Manhattan. Against my
own purposes a pause descends upon me. Deterritorialized within shadows of the
Empire's nerve. 'Urban Pastoral'? — who could stand it?

"The heiroglyphics of destitution."

—Rev. Jesse Jackson

I am that which television won't show. And the whole world slips into my backpack. Cool under a railroad tresfie. Three boys with Louisville Sluggers walking towards the unimaginable baseball diamond. If I could, I'd set Wonder Bread loaves adrift to Ellis Island. The maps stop me. With the triumph of exchange value over use value, all meanings, all lies, become possible. The tribe-of-the-sixties is dwindling. And Grossinger's Hotel offers a "Woodstock Revival Single's Weekend." I'm eating paté off a frisbee. I'm a sponge for duty-free facts. I'm smarter than the average bear. My life is a Tex Avery cartoon. I have travelled this way to spoil the files of decay that spring into this nervous landscape owing nothing but in clips that shine stains across the author's unleavened signature. The twin towers of the World Trade Center symbolize the end of all competition and the end of all original reference. I open a bag of Dipsy Doodles and give each a Christian name. Human consciousness possesses a series of inner genres for seeing and conceptualizing reality. How that twilight in her breasts makes question marks in my throat.

Joel Lewis

"New Jersey is like a derelict California."
—Robert Smithson

The flies are elsewhere. Little eggs nourish me in this scratchy wilderness. Homegrown fortunes are deadly. One can only put a limited amount of one's authentic personality into an apartment. We duck off the road and the cops appear. Cars pass by playing "La Cucaracha" on their horns. I'm swimming in this, really. Functioning wharves resemble crayolas. And then the problem of the people who stand still, weeping. Don't get pissed at the news headlines. Move to Entropia and forget it all. We are not finished, however, even yet, with the complex problem of the pressure to consume. I think I see Black Tom Island. I smell tires broiling over a hickory pit. Arid gazes from everywhere. Homely light and reef rocks. I mount a mound and see the Narrows jammed with tankers. And the Battery seawall. And families on Gates Avenue being families. Speed of the shore is about my eyes. And if this came about by my own ordinal reach, so what? The cues are what counts. And that there is no 'goal.' I'm carving words like a Columbus day turkey. A smokestack out there made out of wallets. We all depart with Jiffy-Pop brains. Privileged latitudes duck the issue. Nothing, nothing it seems, looks like homes.

Main Street, Paterson

Coffee may produce an illusion of alertness,
TV shrinks the world to five basic shots, makes it
gentle on overtaxed brains. On the end of this
street is dappled sky above the Watchungs
& past those mountains
& on all these blocks
dumb ephebe past breathes
nickel smoke on the curbs.

The rooftop squabs sounds a low putter
above Fair Street's West Indies stalls. And. L'Enfant's
imprint remains at the core: circular streets
surrounding the unwashed marble
of the Carrere & Hastings City Hall.

This city choked by its destiny
— short-term Pantheon of the Industrial Past.
This city as walking museum, the ghost factory smoke
caught in my lungs and an entire district
of old silk mills restored to a bright condition
dressed in a false history.

So why am I flustered at the logic of dollar's progress?
I'm full of mist dawn Aprils at the Great Falls'
cusp, and of that cheap marbled notebook
filled with my first writings that bobbed above
the urban limits.

And this redignified waterfall & these reanimated mills
appear as the faded Persia of a once optimistic syntax
we once thought an elegance at least ten years
from this writing, as if plundered
from the core of bright bulb recall.

Joel Lewis

The greed in this geography is what's left
of a contract that is a city,
and of money paying for one's
daily unfinished indignation.

The Track of My Tears

I have come far to fall apart with fits. My hands
time the steps and I start again, restless
among the timid and discrete. It isn't that
monopoly capitalism has done in my brain
but its just that late capitalism irritates
the shit out of me. I am slow to anger & hum along
to the beep of cash registers.

A mystery to me how much simultaneous pain and joy
you find merely circling the block. Take me for a fool
and I'll take you for a dromedary. The subtle interplay
of power and hierarchy piss me off. We work harder
just to stay submerged. Confessions have made
the secretive meaningless. I'm defenseless when too
sure of myself. I try to keep in touch with
everybody. The skyline is all colors, forms
& shades: night's shell of competition.

I came this far to go further. All the music
seems to linger. The diamond fortress wants *YOU*.
The world of the newspaper stand is a dent
in the metropolitan form. I pass the dark shops
of Sunrise Plaza wondering if this is my "homeland."
A compendium of the quotidian equals
relations on a flat plane.

I am a monograph of restoration.

Joel Lewis

After Hearing the Lee Konitz Trio

Shutter phase of Manhattan's nightwork
& the Church Street post office is cluttered with nightmailers.
Shade of terrific things shadowed
by the pulseless surge of memory.
Eighteen years ago, Paterson, in the loft above an IGA market.
"Silk City" ran on minimal efficiency.
And we allowed ourselves nothing of the future.
The music came from somewhere there
and sounded like the back-up band for the Drifters. Nothing
was determined, you were about to go out
and among your heads, your prodromal weather let me
read "vivacious" instead of madness.
Night throb Passaic gogo bar thunk
squanders the recall of "then" the drift
of a "where are they all now."
You last heard in a not-needed call
ten years back, the Weehawken air pebbled
with drifting saucer magnolia petals, not enough
patience with myself, no emotional capital to spare
for the ever-changing economy of insanity.

Algiers

It seems perfect, muted
as a prayer gorgon,
and the rim of the city was a crescent
of RC Colas & melting Moon Pies.
Faulty CD player turns the Meters into John Cage.
Day-Glo bird roosts near the Necco-colored tank.
This is where I invest the habits of my wrist
&, on this swath of levee, krewe-floats
became tips of joy for schoolkids on holiday.

It wasn't in my cards, though,
palming hot sauce in lieu of talisman.
My planet is a crib whose orange juice is gaunt.
I flag down portions of people.
I break bread with a goat who knew Monk.
I don't, then, know anything but the sources.
I check my watch to see when the do-dads hatch.
I have all these rivers running through my shirt.

Birth of The Cool

Call King's Row "small town Freud" and Ronald Reagan's
"WHERE'S THE REST OF ME!" becomes a displacement
of a cigar. We enter the magic magazine to see
Miles Davis' Nonette at the Royal Roost
playing Johnny Carisi's *Israel* on lit cigarettes. Rain
across Duffy Square, no moon nightlight
& the papaya vendors' luau hats have become
soaked clumps of hemp. Now reckless
in the dim room; not a subscriber to nostalgia,
but still trust in the renewal of things.

And after the gig: The broken white lines jump
in front of Lee Konitz as he drives
home in a dark jalopy on the road past
the Tootsie Roll factory.

Lennie Tristano's Subway Stop

The overnight TV news is where they let
ageing newswomen practice their craft
and where anchormen in wheelchairs can speak
of their love for Satie.
This is paradise: A gate.
This is Utopia: A stopwatch.
I worry that my alarm clock will not wake me up.
You know that.
You know that my favorite constellation is Jersey Black.
How do you know if your food is safe to eat?
We took screaming lessons from an opera singer.
*"And I **do** care,"* said The Face.
A planet was shining on me.
The newspaper is so empty that l keep waking up.
I was born with the radio on.
A Velamint bounces off the sewer grate.
Why are there so many tourists in your neighborhood?
Nothing is taken care of.
This is your brain on drugs.
You have settled for the mudbank.
All the world is "out" tonight.

To the Great Hard-Bop Pianists

Club cloakroom as soothing franchise, hats
for men lacking hats, and revise your face
as an authentic Mr. B collar ducks
beyond the reach of a dog-legged street.
I rap at the mystery door, nothing happens.
Phone ring: empty nest. I have all these friends
who keep accurate time.

The tone scientists have returned
from the lab. The reports came in from
the detective books. At home, Bobby Timmons' children
called him: "dear unpasteurized father of the depths."
At the Elysian Cafe's backroom, she told me
of Red Garland's last Dallas years of gamely
playing drunks' requests.

Crushed Marlboros. Good tip in ashtray. Old
sports jacket in an eye-blinking pattern.
Horace Silver runs from us in streams.
Wynton Kelly leaves a gig in a great dark jalopy.
The time machine's habit of summoning up Elmo Hope.
Everything can happen, including Ray Bryant.
Kenny Drew's nervous pulse across a Zildjian's rim,
the light source for the hewed volumes
of scrolls.

The Heavenly Music Corporation

Please sit in the apple juice seat.

Cosmetic laws govern the Aqueduct. Owl deep. If she had known that he was crippled by the collapse of one of his own sculptures, she could never see the work in an objective distance.

I woke up to the grim discovery that I was cast out of the Passaic County poetry community.

Articulation by Charlie Haden. The symbolic must never be confused with the psychological. Tone bags too swift for measure.

Functional ladders of competence. Seeing the Cecil Taylor Unit at the Whitney Museum, 1978. What haunts the system is symbolic demand. Alan Alda a paradigm for the sensitive man?

There's a lot of land in Kansas. Work so monotonous that they hum along with the Muzak attempting to stay awake. Who buys record albums these days?

New windshield wipers satisfy her. The purest grade of rubber bands.

Every summer Nathan waited for "The Cream" to get back together. What's this month's Keith Jarret album? Rosicrucian propoganda relayed on a Fax. New metaphors have the power to create a nude reality. I Love Lucy set back social relations fifty years. Ornette Coleman's silence is fueled by the octane of pride and anger. A syracuse of trombones. New book on American Buddhist scat singers. Levels and degrees of light. Derek Bailey attaches no social value to his art. Okinawa has its own traditions. When architects design homes for their parents. Stylish demarcation. Records you hated but grew to love.

As culture advanced, language made progressively greater use of temporal ideas and less of the spatial.

One can never listen to Rashied Ali on Coltrane's late sessions without thinking of Elvin Jones. No sunset in New York for three days. Stravinsky, hearing the work of a young composer, said to Robert Craft "He's a nice guy — but who needs it?"

Only can describe its contours. Stealing tins of King Oscar sardines as an act of radical kleptomania. Jug-handle turns. He called oversized portable stereos "Third World Suitcases."

Derrida my dreams.

Memory of commercials about eating Jello with chopsticks. Loving Shari Lewis & Lambchop. Legend of Albert Ayler found strapped to a jukebox in the East River. "It's all folks music. I nevah hoid no horse sing!"

This is a Sick Relationship. Just as the hillbilly has no real awareness of the present, they have no grasp of the past. Everybody wants radio cabs. Lennie Tristano recorded the first evidence of "free jazz." Quibbling over Blue Sky Laws.

Bananamoon.

He stalked out of the room when he heard the poem but returned when his friend commented,"If you're *really* such a big Buddhist, it wouldn't bother you so much." Jean-Paul Sartre's favorite jazz artist was Thelonius Monk. Red streaks over Bayonne. Linguaphonic.

Travels to the foreign land of Hoboken. Popular novels are just like movies only that the story is impeded by words. She was hesitant to tell me she was an anthropology major. She was eager to take the "D" train downtown.

I get one more guess.

When the vanguard party split it was revealed that the leader of the Maoist faction enjoyed masturbating at the party headquarters while hitting a brown dachshund with a ping-pong paddle. Schwann Catalog readers voted Arnold Schoenberg the most hated composer of all time. Miles Davis' recreational activities include "laughing at white people on television." My body was eaten by dogs. Fast 'n bulbous. Marking bricks with Crisco to express dissatisfaction with capitalism and reruns of "Dallas." Perogis on roller skates. I am often homesick for the land of pictures. Local office of Borax. In memory of George Jetson. Alice left for an uptown portrait sitting clutching her thick Penguin edition of Herodotus.

Your argument won't hold water. Chicken-fried steaks. I was a pretty good bop drummer. Then I joined Cecil Taylor's group and he ruined me.

Village of consistencies. Never tell your mother she's out of tune. Her father filled in the word baloons for Thor comics. Gil Evans seems to make notes reside in motionless clouds. The hamburger rests as it's being eaten.

Ismuth. Murkin: a pubic hair wig. Shin splints. She's a "Friend of the Zoo." Kungons = Russians.

Palms indelibly stained from too much Lik-M-Aid. Young memories of the Iron Lung. Dusty Springfield: a traitor to her sex? My head is my only house unless it rains.

Back at the Jodo

Man looks at himself in a mirror
& sees a terrier staring back. A normal day
out there, somewhere. I readjust
pocket saver, hear Coltrane cut
the wedding cake on "Out of This World"
in my head and plunge inside
the Jodo, where the house salad
resembles Stan Getz & the soyburger
is served with a side of geiger counter.

Hauntings from old flaneur days of Ted holding
court in the sidewalk café waiting
on a friend to stand him a sandwich
or Jim Brodey forking tempura vegetable "X"
telling wide-eye young poet me
some great & so wild-it-might-be-true story.

My self-determination and bad alchemy
is the marshalling factor that shunts me past
the national cinema of my brain towards
the expert world of the dinner plate.
Tonight: Beef Don; **eat,** fork!

The Dupree Bolton Discography

It was 1937, the last truly beautiful year
to be in Paris . . . or was it
1952, buying teenager cigarettes for Chet Baker
between sets at the Lighthouse
in Hermosa Beach? Whatever the case, Hoboken
is what I think with.

So thank you for that iced latté
& this view of Exchange Place, Jersey City,
in its best across-the-river
anti-Anselm Adams effect.

And l don't know, *what do you do*
when a blimp lands on your mother?
You ask about the page behind the page
& the best I can muster is to
see myself swimmng in Weehaken Cove
having a conversation with a spatula.

Flavor Bud Living

You say: Paul McCartney is slowly
becoming an American Indian.
I say: "The world goes on while you
sleep, you big **fucking** *narcissist!*"
I encounter creels of octopus
& who would play Ted Berrigan
in a Frank O'Hara biopic?
Randy Quaid??? What you retain
is a radiant center fed
by conflicting nerve flashes And I thought
I had problems. How pleasing
to be among myself, an outake from
an unwritten Jim Thompson novel.
As I write for you from here, doves
and macaroni explode all over
these chestnuts of transience. You
sniff the brass knuckles
and wonder. The least we can do is wave
at each other.

Leaving It up to You

Got my clove cigarettes and a hunk
of challah smeared with ersatz butter.
My imagined Jew beanie is warming
my alleged brains
as monochromatic Clarkson Street
looms like an overstuffed burrito.

I can barely describe the sea at night.
It's not that I'm inhibited,
but these subway tokens and bus passes
have made me an urban buoy.

& no allegiance to the ironic nudge
or the laugh-at-them culture
that thickens the curbs like pine tar.
Good science can't help this subset.
Click tape ON / play Albert Avler to observe.
The nation of footfall around me thickens
fades to my brand of black.

At The Melville Room

The only trace of sabotage, a writing life.
And the acceptance of a personality continues, cattycorner
from the doors of Housatonic Savings. Just spare me the sponge,
the lackings still swing from the popular season.
Nickel-plate perfume is the compass,
a vanished tribe of Meso-Americans are the last
first people They talk large as the life, clutch
Statue of Liberty dolls — their singular gift
from the Burger Zones.

Leaf-brown desk, one scrimshaw bandelore,
old upscale maps that sap the crazy alphabet fractures
& then let the eyes get on with the drenching of thought.
You were born to be a brain, now lost on a haj
with the weenies who stole the initial rhythm germ.

The wax paper world is here
& I have to keep paying tribute while
its nations disintegrates. Eyes divide
verging towards the rootwash
of November's fuzzy trees,
but the land is as vast as the arrangement
of absolute daybreak. The dependable habit
turned him to cargo's cop, dead afternoons
remembering the once world
between window & Greylock.

What's left then?? Space-age hard-hats?
Sounds of carrots hitting ice water?
Pressure pants bursting in poignant reflection? —
A sunny interval is the integrity
of any given false day
& resistance to family's mention
is a brittling effort, the life story
as deep as sprats on the dinner plate.

Some bearded man tapes a hopenote to a desk's lid.
Inaudible creeping drowns his former pride. He files
the pictures of America in his seaman's chest, while
books exercise their surfaces of regret & as the words
name their own displacements.

An archetypal question?
— The entire dark nothing else
outside, hungering.

Iron Path

for David Shapiro

October Sunlight.
A thin event.
Milk-glass on
diner formica.

A child's calm relation
to his Mother.
Half-empty milk-glass.
Thin boy under sunlight.

This emphasis on
facts & cheerful moods.
The payphone rings.
Thin shower of things.

Milk.
Meat another luxury.
Rain fell in a mass.
Mother & her tabloid.

Rumbles of gossip.
Earmarked overnight virtusosity.
The Woman is making a list. Enough
of the initial recognized melody.

Milk dries in the glass.
Sentences get no closer than "this."
Menu's brimming calligraphy.
1954 miracle: "dry onion soup."

Arriving at the very
moment that power
marries power. Day forced through
a watch. Tawny curb.

The Woman draws a new list.
France: its regional cheeses.
Payphone ringing.
The velcro icons.

Payphone ringing: beauty of neglect.
Sunlight on turbinado sugar.
Mother orders coffee buns.
The Woman begins a new list.

Kafka wanted to entitle his *oeuvre*:
"Attempts to escape the paternal sphere"
Sun's luck to triumph.
Continual punctures on the world.

Newspapers hint at dark property.
Muzak's middle Dylan recreations.
Truck brake screech mirrors Coltrane's trills.
The Woman lists the dinner guests.

Capitalism's mineshaft of useful exagerrations.
That story is finished. Sunlight nears
a backroom of badmen. She asked
for a glass of water. Thin shower, things.

"The glass of milk" is a non-verbal experience, right?
Child picks at a BLT. A delicate instinct.
Factoids on the surface of the world.
Chance movements in a river.

Supply the ancient customs.
Hot griddle dents air with a sizzle text.
African prow on the granite frigate.
To live in a city is to cross the street.

The icy solitude of the laughing woman.
Enough of the original melody remains for
recognition. Sunlight reaches mother's
shoulders. Balking at pushing on.

The trick: blow out the candles
without getting burned. Child yanks out
a gadget: playtime. Public spaces: the daily
museum. Debate among catastrophes.

Which speaking subject said that?
F-hole guitar, dusty. The great
theatre of human studies. The fury of
an ice cream vendor on a frigid day.

Rubber-necker picks up payphone's receiver.
Man's Voice. Click. Tone.
Bullies have traditionally been concerned
with the beating up of sissies.

A certain chord makes the home vanish.
The hash slinger's dream of darts.
Mother pays the check. Change dribbles
across the table. The Protegé enters.

I'd like to thank the little people who made
all this possible. The bus-boy removes
the milk glass. Tip of the tongue phenomenon.
Mother and Child passing a broken window.

Whole economies based on the market value
of S'Mores. Franks and beans: "Hounds
on a island" in early thirties diner parlance.
Which speaking subject said "that."

The Woman is drowning in lists.
Each pencil an armature. Old boy network.
A digital watch on par with trousers. An omelette
is a straight blank whole. Pinholes called movies.

Waiters chant the ancient dirge.
The sheet of shadows command attention.
The Woman departs. Goat-invented "coffee."
Neither feeder nor dreamer be.

The hiss of thick slice bacon.
The Protegé's frayed velveteen car coat.
The curious cold side of Milt Jackson.
The Woman passing Mother & Child. Bustop.

The residual bitterness in being
a mere heliotrope. The air fixes a salutation.
Reconstructed bus approaching. The Woman enters
her car. Imagine a slender world's exit. A busstop.

Write the history of a time zone. Lunch crowd.
The skin *really* writes. The half-life
of a Majority Whip. Broadcast
the enablers of success. A "sammich."

Spam, invented in 1936, is the food
of Post-Modernism. Mother & Child in
departure. Ladies & Gentlemen, The Woman has left
The Poematorium! Ancient earth's helpless chatter.

The sun reflects attentive hands.
Winter hardens the judgement of the séance.
Who dare criticizes the lunch one has
while on safari? Tender pictures of a once family.

Coded in the many waves of absence and departure.
Two miles from the diner: a payphone is ringing.
Stoplights are The Child's personal
monsters. Mother winces. Nervous hands.

The Protegé in intermission from split pea soup.
Pure pitch hiss of a chili fart.
All margins resemble pitchblende.
Ambushed facts in every corner.

Curb produces unleashed powers.
Inside the bus, The Child was adding up
the many detours. Each pencil an
old boy network. Buses *are* unbarbered tanks.

Joel Lewis

At the border of a public-use boundary.
The Woman's thumping heel. "Ladies" were once
a Third Force. The Mother's behavior could be
characterized by transitive verbs.

If the words are successful, the Protegé
survives. The Child had cried for his
coloring book. Sunlight shone on a wedge
of the Hashslinger's apron. Alter the bare traces.

You can't make a silk purse from scrambled eggs.
Tree-lined street hierarchy. Laughter
is benign censorship.
Three miles from the diner: Spam sammich.

How the dictionary valorizes speech.
An imaginary thin world, here. Radio waves
as the lipstick trace of the culture. A sign
below the cash register: *Gloating Prohibited,*

Decay is the outcome of need.
Soft-white bulbs reflect upon the milky coffee.
October is not displaced. Factory district's
smoke chorus. The Spoils. Not the little dots.

Is, Was (Changing)

for Christopher Wilmarth

Doubloons nudge the pocket,
crazy fuel lifts the experience
of investigative reports. These pictures
convey nothing but plantains that detonate
from time to time. I open the glass brick door
& encounter pencil. Is it possible that anorexia
plagues women firefighters? Sunball against
the Second Watchungs as it drags East Orange
into the ooze below the Jersey crust. The configurations
and proportions of place evoke
human presence. That feeling is intimate.
You are acknowledged.

Joel Lewis

Cool Blue Halo

DarJeeling tea for you, Java mud on my end
of the marble table. A pagoda cloud hovers
above the street and seems
lit by the heavy wattage
of the Samsung display.

Let's try to imagine fish cat-
napping under thick Antarctic ice
or, going to the interior, Little
America's Admiral Byrd almost
dispatched thanks to a faulty
kerosene stove.

Does anything register? Living a life of
serene vegetation wasn't in our cards,
nor money,
        status
             or prestige.

Fame still seems a hopenote.
But, how to get it or what it really is
besides a brief glare of exultation.
Though you have chosen the path
of mystery woman, I'll throw mental
pokerdice to propose that you suffered
the same teenage intellectual's high school
hell as I did.And though your Doris
Humphrey to my R. Crumb wouldn't have
amounted to a hill of tofu
in those minnow years,
here we are: still friends & never lovers, on
opposite ends of the gender gully.

Today, on the centenary of the battle between
John L. Sullivan & Gentleman Jim Corbett
I feel the need for a handler & a cut man
to pop out from behind Dean & DeLucca's
brass cappuccino cauldron.

And I'm sure you feel those days, too
in this land of gaps and cold objects. But
a neon chromoscope assures future good
weather & we're just too far away to read
the calamitous newsband events ripping
about #1 Times Square

& can we ever forget what we now know that we
didn't know then? Against the bagatelle winds up
Damon Runyon Way, we are writing
the handbook for a country beyond
the purchase of the murderous daily
income of sympathy.

Mechanical Weathering:
Paterson Scanned Postcards

Sun's gloves a glow on shorthand curbs   face-off with city's   wrecked image
Seems Play-dough with typewriter   chatter like a wreck from the powerful
mirror of a wish
    or from behind Hinchecliffe Stadium walls

Auto parts in whorls   Water curved these walls in the glow
of superb handwriting   Irish angry machine, Paterson's own:
"ta' blow da English Navy ta' Hell!"   Years as backyard whale
First $ale: His Majesty's WWI fleet — no gain —

Rubber (Pennsy Pinky) ball enters poem   Early March/brisk picnic
Pentecostal Spanish families enter with mirage map smiles
Mother with surrogate bairn trots through the chasm's mist
Talked in words: repeat America's Code: How clever & divisible

So severe heads soften us for marching orders.
Sounds of Keno machines at TILT   not human shaped
Winterdirt on Cianci Street bodegas like so many
soda crackers............. the second they hit the soup.

The Book of Daylight that is the Great Falls. A man from Linden
cracks the subset. Old Doc Williams (ghost in machine): a flop
like Olson claimed in Mayan Letters?   Sez "O": Dumb
sincerity do him in — in different voices.

Nervous & unattended fried chicken shack   Hollow silk mills create
reciprocal decay   Pen competes against cascades
    Call it a "vestibule"   Two lonely kids
Lou Costello sleeping on a lobby sofa (Hamilton Hotel, c. 1939)

Native chlorine stuck to slickery paths
Stupid bloody Tuesday?
    Every dime is consciousness
You must always start with something   Bus axle snaps

Love knot earrings in a joyeria window
Low plateau parallels my white-skin privilege face.
Lull between   jack-hammer blunderbuss
                The prominent names.

Laboring at the reader-response text.   Is there a Fish
in these Falls? Okay, Lunch!!   "Better qualified" means
better equipped for domination   My fan club waits me
or build me up buttercup!   A milky cloud above Garret Mt.

Minutes to access capital's damage   & most people personify it
as "LIQUID TERROR"   "This is the first clock in Paterson
that had Arab numerals"   Stood here steady upon this
morning roof as no more than a piece of the puzzle.

Graffiti at Libby's Lunch: "Nelson is a *FAGGOT*
& lost his CPA license, TOO!"   Civil War caused
by a broke traffic box   Each stoop
one part of the city's original name.

Later, it's lunch   & the poem points
towards the domestic life   So weave a parable through this
Book of Daylight   Sheer memory: Another government-in-exile
              All these buildings dressed in the same history.

Ever wonder where your garbage goes? Last red ash
of a condensed Marlboro growing dim on
the borderline grate of catchbasin. Certain themes are
incurable, endless, unenviable.

Tranquil men sit on the grey-coated curbs waiting
Opening Day (baseball!!)   "Capitalism begins
when you open the Dictionary" (S. McCaffery)
     Study the marginal notes scribbled onto a greenback.

Is this the bridge where Ginsberg first jacked-off under?
     Flat tomes in the afternoon   That a city itself is a dog!
                    Or Else: LUNCH!
Bleary uphill shadows   Urban tableau's dementia.

Go-bots run this city   Chemicals can not create
disharmony when one's orchestra
is out of tune   A city is a big job
already forgotten

"Friendship Dinner": Paterson institution, stacked beefsteaks amid old guys'
gladhands   Fear is the only emotion
that has no music   This simple interior contains urinals with
ice-cubes as primitive Sani-pucks

Words meander through too many city streets   & the vast
network information mulch relieves us of the responsibility of having
to "know" anything   Sunlight on a churchwoman's bulky pocketbook
            3 lonely boys   Dime on a gumspot

One step ahead of the brain police   Cottage cheese platter
at Meyer Brothers' old-timey luncheonette.
            Has he "earned that last line, class?"
Not determined by what I've recently read.

Information: Any difference that makes a difference. (G. Bateson)
        in 1828 Paterson gave America its first factory strike
when cotton workers quit the looms protesting a change
in the Lunch Hour   This city full of links.

"The looms run us!" Toward nightfall the birds gradually settle
on the narrow ledges below the small domed
City Hall   "Big Bill" Haywood walking down Market Street, his
one eye fixed on the crowd of strikers waiting his appearance

The horizon suggests the plain fact of suburbs   Opinions
rendered by the power station that is the curbs
        Holland's *Fenian Ram* submarine sunk in collision
with the Weehawken Ferry   Ancient urban earthworks

Coffee the shade of a boiled lobster.
            Young Ginsberg in school, right hand
high filled with the "correct answer"   Smiles exchanged
on Ellison St.: parody of conviviality commences

A wolf-pack of crypto-sissyboys head towards the Danforth Library's
"cool of books"   Bo Diddley's "Who Do You Love?" accompanies a mangle
dancing at the Lou Costello Rec Center.
                    Are these of great importance to the nation?

Black Muslims hit the street   Dark are needs and how unfulfilled is this
dreaming for their arrival
                    The F. W. Woolworth is actually only
an armband of the "Drearily Autonomous Consumer"   Prominent Name.

He finally threw in the towel with his attempts to apply
Magic Realism to his South Paterson neighborhood   "As where
you begin": possible meaning of Totowa, section of Paterson.
                    Low on exact bus change.

Hot newspaper change placed square in palm
by the blind courthouse Korean Vet news vendor
                    Wobblies from a dream.
Cataract's spring trance.

Late afternoon sun is slants on a patient in
an upstairs Market Street office.
          The Whopper takes four pickle slices.
Resemblance is not a thing to feed.

Be the city, rename its streets — then leave.
     The radical engagement of a dead-end job.
          The Pennsy Pinky is about to hit the catchbasin grate
          Reinterpret your last 3 days.

Birch beer on tap all over this city's many bars.
The city can be one's personal whale.
               The author of *The Book of Daylight*
is at Borders this afternoon   Driven back in a coughing taxi.

Scary: a payphone ringing, no one around to get the call.
     Old money seems spiked in the double reflection of writing
     The simple power in female presence.
Landscape pickled with the full cadence of its history.

The porkpie hat as a souvenir or gravity
　　　　Beery uphill shadows at twilight on Belmont Ave.
　　Narrow cracks between slabs elucidate the possibility
of a predecessor non-city.

Treated as leper by ex-friends when entering
the camphor-ball air of Haledon Pub　　　Not determined
by what I've recently read　　Pastry Wagon outside the Unemployment
Office; one Hispanic family sharing a small custard pie.

"To live in a city until it becomes alien to you" (E. Canetti)
　　　　We burn to the echo of the past that Paterson drowns in.
Ether elevator music in the halls of Mayer Bros. Department Store.
　　This city once full of "pinks"

Class tour of the Market Street McDonald's　　The steady beat of pocket change told
them that Al was coming up the block
　　　　Traffic lights changing under midday sun
More and more faces recall other faces

　　　In a rainstorm, people look as if their lifeplans had been
shattered a long, long time ago　　Always pursued by slender distractions,
his continued feeling　　　　as brainless as a biscuit

Machine Made of Words Dept: We now say "he has a bad chip" instead
of "he has a screw loose."　　This city in an intimate physical
place, a whole hotel striding towards better fortune　　　The asceticism
of a streetcleaner as goes he about his job.

Cryptic slopes of raw nerves that's people jockeying for a lunch hour stool at
Paterson's madbar of wildbars in immaculate winter faces of red raw cheeks &
skyblue lips (homage to Kerouac).　　"Advance the Cinema!" his wife shouts.
Buying Cheez-Its with food stamps

The store clerks gather at the entrance in their blue smocks, waiting for the
manager to let them in　　Danforth Library as a grey battleship in the heart of
Paterson's think winter of poverty
　　People's faces read as "panic"　　Exploding cherry bombs

Imagine a city reduced to a shoebox full of postcards.........
    The soup kitchen is full of empty tureens & turns away the 22 men still left
standing on line   Most of today's poetry suggests no locality but ego
ten minutes too late for Egg McMuffins

Hot game of stoop ball on Straight Street   The hopeless task
called flyfishing in the Passaic River   Revamping
the McDonald's coffee stirrer to end use as a poor man's
coke spoon   Crude combustion of light

"The reading of this city you've made
is possible; but it still rains
at the scene of writing" (*Book of Daylight*).
    Mustard as motley accouterment to the Texas Hot Wiener.

"AM I STARTING TO LOOK LIKE A NORWEGIAN TO YOU, BWANA?!" (Mayor
Wassail to angry mob at a City Council meeting)   Call the Great
Falls of the Passaic a "sluice of dreams" & admire
what you've written   Yet another phantom diurnal moon

Dare Paterson the task to exist in time   Severe heads behind
the counter of the Unemployment Office   The complained of the Buick's severe
condition, yet they drove with him to the top
of Garret Mountain   A cold bottle of sacramental Pepsi

Again & again: city as a trough for facts & observations
            Passaic's water smooth as witnessed
Garret Mountain as an alp at the end of Cianci Street.
    A blur of languages, and not at all a system of languages.

The diminished urban sphere & the dream of augury.................
            Waking up with the television on.
        Laying in bed, at night in his Main Street loft, the word "FAILURE"
rose from his mind & onto the ceiling.

M. Bakunin........ please call home   while walking along
Vreeland Avenue, the store's big flat roof was a particular joy.
        "I don't like men who quote their wives"
Post-Modernism began when McDonald's banned jukeboxes ('56).

East Side High kids dub the House of Shih (local Chinese takeout)
"The House of Shit"   A severing of intention leaves Paterson
          as an orphan signifier.
The gentle world of rubble.

The more that silence surrounds the worker & his alienation,
the more the intellectual feels obligated to provide
meaningful social commentaries.   Gnawing at some gizzards
from Kansas Fried Chicken.   We were the loveliest human snow.

The audience was respectfully submerged at the end
of the Kung-Fu film festival.   Street-family sharing a box
of Post Toasties.   And *another* painting of the Great Falls!
     Poet "B" waiting for rejection letters in morning's mail.

Eating a sloppy, onion-drenched Hot Texas Wiener
destroys the filmy boundary between
self-consciousness & abandon.   You learn to feel so completely
out-loud in a crowd of noonday browsers.

New film at the Kung-Fu Theater: *In the defiles of the Signifier!*
          The transcultural information found
in layered urinal graffiti.   I always seem to be wrapped
  in the melodrama of vulgarity.

The spoon collection of the Passaic County Historical Society.......
          Often lively & realistic, usually not as good as TV.
     The wind sucks up ripe debris.
               Glistening puddle water.

          Out of snow, you can't make cheesecake.
He dreamt of his grandfather, the angry Italian anarchist
loom-worker.   Another
immigrant family from a nonscheduled Oceanic land.

     City as a public goon show. Fast summer thunderstorm pours
through the broken window of the long-empty Akont Mills.
     A possible sour smile from a machinelike face.
To have money is good; to control money is still better.

An old man thumbs his paperback copy of *The Book of Daylight.*
   "Try to set the night on fire!": where'd I heard that, a wisp
of music from a old blue Valiant zooming past me
on Goffle Brook Road   Farting is a sign of aggression.

The townspeople had one comprehensive explanation
for all these singularities. The Haledon-bound bus greatly
reminded me of my cave-dwelling childhood.
         All these names. . . translated into Double-Dutch.

My father-in-law bailed the Pep Boys out a financial jam.
               Seems an Ugly People Contest
on the streets tonight   Dare Paterson
the hard task of existing in time   & in the gentle world of rubble.

"Once we were one with our Dreams," sd the old Italian anarchist.
         She is naked in the heart of her words.
      Polite children swimming at the Lou Costello Public Pool.
      The particular cigarette smoked by Paterson politicians.

            Adventist lightning erupting outside
the blood serious storefront baptistery.
      The upside down laugh called fast foods. God created a world
that is full of many little worlds (*Book of Daylight*)

Indeed, it is so nice to hear of that lucky so & so who manages
to outrun his/her dreams.   Fresh supply
of Duncan Return Tops (Yo-Yo's) at the Dominican Bodega.
      Some tepid rain above this sheer municipal loss.

Tooth decay was once known in Paterson as "Pastry Wagon Molars."
A heritage shrub on the gangster's lawn.
         Arguing about the exact point of Bud Powell's decline.
Lathered & ready for another day's abuse.

   The throng eddies away,
            & carries them asunder.
History is imbedded in each item we touch.
               Street jive as noontime pie.

Each night, he tries to forget about his adopted city
by playing Righteous Brothers albums
& crying softly.
Whispering sternly & significantly among the powerful of a city.

Painting a watercolor to be called "Still Life with Sweet 'n Low."
The encampment of the indigent has come for us.
Dwelling among totem traffic boxes. I sense the ghosts
of the people who once rented this apartment.

Elaborated spaces are the pleasure
of a city   These mills are the result
of the intensity in space   How it all looks
atop Garret Mountain: a whole emergence, a grid.

Nervous Fabric

for David Meltzer
and
for Melvin Bukiet

First order: wire test.
Sun's luck
to triumph. I'm off
to the edge, here. A half
empty can of Cel-Ray. A worn
Talmud, ready for burial. I came
from Spain a long time ago. Now:
a nickel drops onto the curb
of Washington Street. Young
punk mankind.. In the air:
the imaginary balloons
of false sight.

Someone is out there surfing
on sine waves, but that person
isn't me. Me is standing in
for the lice in the spotlight. That
isn't morose fact — it's moonlighting
in the domain of late capitalism. A quick
kiss to the mezuzah doorpost
                              & this absolutely
competent hand reaches into a pocket
to pay for more fuel for dreams.
                    I once took up the clarinet.
                    My holiday in risk.
Dear Monad: *Do I have to spell it out for you?*

Joel Lewis

World gone
kabuki.   Bus goes
bump, full with bus-pass women in
hair-styles of their TV favorites.
            Summer in Hoboken is the season
for random Yuppie beatings, I'm up to my neck
in my incompletions. The link between

                        money
                                    &
                                    words:

    ground
            zero
                    of
                        modern
                                    society

Welcome to the atmosphere
along the shirtside of the street

You can pit the walls, you can chew
the yellow pencil into the surface
of a Manhattan avenue.   Experience
                              is a form of paralysis.
Water is another matter. A quarter
goes into the *tzedakah* box because it was found
in an unexpected place. Hold me harmless
from grammarians and the beat cop.
                         And with the intensity of a dollar,
I arrive to listen. In full light
of day, I manage to walk and chew
Dentyne at the same time.

Eating my mother's chopped liver
hurts my teeth. Another ferry docks in Hoboken without
me on board. "AARRRGGHHH" said the pirate.
Why? Arguing the virtues of Charlie Parker's
output on Verve records, we were reduced
to carjacking one another.
                            Nations await my industry.
I consult the targum and surface knowing
less than water. Nothing on the World Band tonight
except **"Goat Herder's Jamboree"**
from Radio Tirana. New Jersey is wedged
between the setting sun and a newer form
of geography. The secret
to writing wonderful poetry, Elizabeth, is simple:

1) Never go below a self-set level.
2) Have the certainty and doggedness of Ed Woods, Jr.

       . . . . . . The rest is commentary.

Out of unemployment comes
self-employment. I woke up
in a backroom
where the glass is thinner. I yawned
and ordered strong coffee.
So many people out there
doing desperate work.
I want the kind
of information that can't be
melted into E-Mail. And I won't
read a poem that wasn't
written indoors. Candor ends paranoia. *
Grammar says: "What, me worry?"

---

*—Allen Ginsberg

Anxiety is truly my device, it's part
of a Masoretic inheritance that
I schlep into this parkland
of bribed souls.
                    Languages dream
in derision. Rooms contradict
the dead weight of fatigue. There
goes a Mr. Softee truck, a semi-sacred site
exposed by daily use. Time to repair
the face of circumstances. Please don't
tell me about your life.

A relief
to open
a book of poetry
     & to find
yourself in the presence
of a brain. Now I pledge
allegiance to the American sentence,
invest in that war of attrition called
a Jamaican beef patty
        & think about
the history going on above this aquifer.
I have no privilege to renounce, only
minor bits of accommodation.
At its worst, poetry can be best defined
as an emotional retrieval system.
The world rolls on as you sleep.

Joel Lewis

Drifting off again as the "E" train
heads under the East River. Little
rubbed-in messages everywhere. What
we *really* need now are fewer *hints*.
        I dream of a lake. A voice surfaces
not calling my name. Unsure
of what is inside the canopy beneath the brittle
crust of a Hot Bean Pie, I let it go
unpurchased. I put in a job application
for the position of a "laughing stock." Who is above
this tunnel? My friends want to go
to hell in a handbasket, but with
dignity. I'm vehemently and sincerely
part of this geography.

Recognition is incidental.
The city full with men carrying
lunch pails, wearing bleak
haircuts. Call it
tribal refusal, or just
getting the "bugs" out of It.

   First: the empty subway station,
   calculated through the mechanics
   of risk. Then memories
   of the Maxwell House factory on
   a humid night, Hoboken's seasoned air
   stained by caffeine.

Bring your bottle of schav along, we'll
use it as whole oil. The opposite
is what I intended. These wrinkled brown houses:
not Zion. Another day in the diaspora.

Joel Lewis

We are equally disloyal
in our good hats. 1968:
World on fire. The Yeshiva of Hudson County.
Tractate Bava Metzia — parsing out the obligations
in the situation of when your neighbor's cow
slips in your cow's shit
and breaks a leg.

"I don't have a cow!
Nobody here has a cow! We're Jews,
not farmers!" shouted Mark Mendelowitz,
son of a reformed rabbi.
                              Our teacher, Rav Krut, was silenced.
I guess It was heresy. But nobody ever quite
put it that way above the din
of the Public Service buses
leaving next-door's depot
for the late-afternoon rush-hour.

I'm doing chump-change teshuveh when
I tell you-the-reader that I apologize
for any poems of mine
that you did not like.
                    In Europe, the most
obstreperous nations are those
most addicted to coffee. I understand
the boredom of clerks, but do clerks
understand the interpersonal boredom
of social workers? Boom of pregnant cave dwellers.
I smell honeycake. Of poet "X" it was
noted: "Her childhood was like so many
oatmeal cookies." I need some sort of mammoth syrup
and a calming dream about
the Straits of Oman. Down below,
woodcarvers are on their way
to forests full of wardens.

In Cyprus, if you happen to be
in a strange village
and sit in a coffee shop, you will
probably find that your coffee
has been paid for
by someone else.

The morning music is Terry Riley
& the money is already being counted
        So you, you & you, FOLLOW ME!
Let's find a website for the emotionally challenged
& set up shop. The world's annual
coffee production is a volume equal
to the hourly outflow of the muddy Mississippi.

Saluggi's rules were simple:
toss around the wool watchman's cap
of the most nebbishy boy in the class.

Rain prints its tiny pressure on my scalp.

Punk architecture and the rest of the world
that remains in a rut. The speaking men
have gone to sleep. Wooden stirrer
into my grand latté, novel
no more, capitalism of the barristas
and their wardens, the mood music
puffing up behind the marble wall. Daily
riverfront life has me dreaming
of trollies over Weehawken Cove
                & no matter which way l hold
the maps, the votes get counted
the same way. Love. Gloom. Cash. Love.

The Journal Square bus is so⁻
rickety, I can barely hear myself
getting depressed! In Florida, a hurricane
advances on a spinach salad abandoned
by its eater. I cast my net for coffee,
settle for Big Eyed Beans From Venus served
by barristas wearing plane hats.
            Evening in Hoboken, endless
shoelaces on the feet of commuters.
"Gimmee a cup of heaven acid," said
the Billy Joel fan. Succos is nearly here,
& I walk along Observer Highway
with lulav and etrog mumbling brachas.
I want to sleep beneath a tabernacle, a
booth, an anti-fallout shelter, something
that gives even odds on seeing
the morning star.

            Joel Lewis

Rabbis invade my mind to sell me
the secrets of pure alliteration.
        I kill time staring skyward
at the stucco. I pass up espresso
for congoleum. I shop
at Macy's and buy
a private language kit
        & just who **ARE** these baby
Language poets and what do they want
from me? Younguns, believe me, there
once *was* a band called Pablo Cruise
        & people bought their records. Years
ago, I promised myself weapons which wouldn't
weigh me down and settled
        for the chuck steak of discernment.

He
    used
        to be
           a good
               friend
                  of
                     mine

but
    he
        went
           and
           stole
               my
                  trouser
                     pockets

. . . translated fragment
(a popular Yiddish folk song that
my father remembers from
a Polish childhood)

Joel Lewis

Sleep
       faster

We need
 the pillows

(Yiddish aphorism)

The worm in horseradish
who thinks
he's in heaven
is only expressing
the worm's capacity
for imagination

(Yiddish Aphorism)

Joel Lewis

You
     can't
dance
     at
two
     weddings
with
     one
behind*

*(tuches)

(Yiddish folk wisdom)

It is forbidden
to cross the road
to meet the man
who is your debtor
    & who you know
can not pay you;
    for it is as it
he were tortured
with fire and water.

(From the *Talmud*: Berachat 66)

Joel Lewis

Thinking about those slippered
professors in their millionaire
hotels as I get ready
tor a future exile. The small fry 'round here
call me 'Diaspora Joe.'

   & I swear by the Temple Service
that you only need a minyan of one
for poetry, so boot it all
& put on a gimmee cup bearing
the image of the martyred Rabbi Akiva.

            I'm talking Jew to you,
Senôr Farrakhan. The paper shredders
are running overtime, the debts mount
and letters oo unanswered. I'm in the gutter,
not because of my religion, but because
I love the word *GUTTER*, it is almost as good
a word as *jalopy*.

So capitalism is really only the burden
of bad options, but what can I really do
except send out salutations
in my eyeblink corduroy car coat.
            The rhythmic torpor
of the CD disk spinning in the player
is on the menu. A blintz surges up
among that which is labeled "thought"
here at the dharmadatu. Strange voices
sing among the planets, a bus bounds
into a Manhattan pothole
& is never seen again.
            I'm sitting still more than
anything else, tugging at my tzitzits
to ward off mental buccaneers.

    In some dark shithole of a lecture hall
    learning commences
    in a cadence of ceremony.

Today is Succos, so I put my cowboy hat on as l eat
sans roof. Everyone in the sukkah smiles at me knowing
what they know, which is something I don't
know and which they won't tell me, because I am in a Stetson
and not a yarmulke. I have taken my real face with me.
I am shaking the lulav and etrog to no purpose other than
it's Succos & I am in the Sukkah eating one boiled potato
under Jersey chemical blue sunset in my ten gallon hat.

What's a cubit?

We are here in a waterfront city celebrating a harvest festival. **What
is Neroli?** Arthur Waskow calls the Sukkah an anti-fallout shelter,
comforting the secular ones who wonder what this all means, USA/'99/CE.
My real face is framed by a cowboy hat. l am shaking
the lulav and etrog. A citron. **Machha Bracha!**

There is no reason to do "it"
or not to do "it"
                    as when you lived
along the sloppy banks of the Passaic
sharing meals with Circassians
& living dishonestly
as a senior urban planner.
                              I have cat dander
in my pockets and command
imperative actions in
a borrowed language
        & when I knead this lump
of air with words, I get a dial tone
for my troubles. Rainbows, letters and acts of writing
were created at twilight on the first
Erev Shabbat. Slice me some
show bread, **Bwana!** No one ever said
to his fellow: *This place is too crowded*
for me to stay here, in Jerusalem.

Part of our history shows that miracles
are a minor part of the parade. Jews do not
believe because of miracles; however, it is our faith
which leads us to read our historical experience
as miraculous.
                I have not yet spoken of the sea,
& do not intend to do so. On Halloween,
I came dressed as a human being.
            And of the assembled signs.
I mimicked a salt bagel. Old Hoboken shul
a Pentecostal temple — where did
those Jews go? No one applauds
the page. The newspapers get printed
in magnetic ink. Nothing is beneath doing
to one who knows what needs to be done.

One of the most distinct
memories that my father has of his
childhood in shietl Poland is when
Zev Jabotinsky came to his village
to hold a rally.

My father's older brothers were Bundists
and spent the day before the rally collecting
rocks to throw at the "Jewish brownshirts."
There was a riot that evening between Jabotinsky's
followers and the Bundists. The Polish
muzikhs were astonished. Jews, who faced daily
relentless anti-Semitism, usually put on a united front.
Now, they were throwing rocks at each other,
shouting **"FASCIST"** at their co-religionists.

Jabotinsky died of a heart attack in Queens not long after.
He was in America trying to raise funds for Jewish refugees.
His last words were a request to be buried in the future
Jewish state. Which was denied by Ben-Gourion, who even
hated him as a corpse. Only when Jabotinsky's disciple,
Menachim Begin, took office were his bones
removed from the boro of cemeteries and interred
in Jewish soil with full state honors.

(11/5/95)

The voices of the Jewish poets
of medieval Spain talk us in
to Zion. Diaspora Joe, you revel
in the pukelands of the West,
yet you dream of the East.
                    Do you enjoy working
in the service of the Philistine,
the Hittite and Hagar's pissed-off
sons? Burn your CPA license, fellow kike
and follow the lead of the Professional
Insane Backpacker in the next
commuter train seat and leave
the precincts of privilege. No
one can be successful
in the company of the insane
unless he converts to insanity.
The Ammonite,
The Moabite,
& Hagar's bitter children
glorify themselves in vision
because of *you,* Diaspora Joe.

(From the Hebrew of Judah Ha-Levi)

Mitzvahs are a problem. There are so
many of them. Jewish law
is a science of mitzvahs. We repeat
our conversations
in the liberating dark.

I cannot remember the precious things I once
saw on television. A few friends, but they
are pissed at me & won't return my calls.

The daily universe is a handful of someone else's
chump change. You, too, wonder about
all this freon? Keep it all on the cuff, but
keep doing mitzvahs silently. **Go ahead Izzie!**
Hit 'em in the kishkas!! Tip the Zoroastrian
hat check girl and step out of Club Arcana
into the deep seltzer of the sages.
Yo! People of Chelm! Follow me!

Catch my breath long enough to witness
the peccadillos of the minor characters
in the human drama. Sun zoom spark.
           A not-quite Maccabee rings the bell asking
for donations. I shut it and say, "Shalom,
ASSHOLE!" Gestures change into
experience. The traffic lights of Europe
maintain the finite. My mind
is as selective as a sewer.
                The ancient rabbis
commended all acts for the public good;
this included lighting dark alleys
& filling ruts in the road.

Our emancipation will not be complete
until we are free of the fear
of being Jews.
                The audience preoccupied
with hand jive. Quiet days along
the Palisades, evenings taken up with questions
of near-revolution and thermidor.
                        Why not syrup into
the defiles of western history? Our child
secular humanism the brat
of nasty indigenous America.
                Got my yarmulke working. It was called
a "Jew beanie" by Italian kids
& slapped off my head on occasion
& I got punched in the head
if I suggested
that Pope Paul the 6th himself
wore the same type skull cap.

                Assimilation is evaporation.

Shemmai says:
                "Love work
                        hate authority
                don't get chummy
                        with the police."

Better a combative sage
                    than a friendly fool
Some voices speak as if on the verge
of saying something useful, the saxophonist
slips in an allusion to Monk in his
solo & the full house goes
stark, art overturns lethargy,
lethargy at the core of our damaged
lives.

      An Ohio Hillel offers backrubs
      & aromatic oils to lure in
      assimilated Jews;
              the Maccabees
      would have slayed them as Helenizers,
      I'd suppose.

A quip collected by one of the scribes
of the Warsaw Ghetto: "We eat
            as if it were Yom Kippur, sleep
            in Sukkahs and dress
            as if it were Purim."

Those fires rustle
dreams, only there
is no light.

"What is a cubit"? she
said. Certain letters and words
have deeper meanings than
others. The rabbi greets his
long-lost sister at the airport,
then states: "Good to see you.
But I must go back to my study.
I have many things to accomplish today."

The text is flooded by its commentary.
It surfaces momentarily, but is crowded
out by its interpretation.
                              Light counts
for something. **What's a cubit, bwana?**
Memory packs the brain's auditorium.
I imagine a *ner tamid* illuminating
a globe of rare metals.

Joel Lewis

Channukah is *not* Jewish Christmas. There ain't
no Channukah bush on the evening stage & only
clear intent avoids the making of oily latkes. In
medieval times, Channukah was a memorial
to the martyrs of the Syrian occupation. Lodged
in the head: the tale of the anonymous family
of martyrs, 7 sons and a mom; each tossed
into a giant FRYING PAN for upholding the faith.

In America, no one knows you
or who your people are or if you
are Kohen or Levite. Nobody knows
from sacrifice or self-sacrifice. Look,
people up and down the streets
have decided to buy radios to
drown out the world.
Don't blame them for this
blame me, blame me and my bad
faith and lack of a stratagem
to fill my pants pockets with shekels
and zlotys. It is mostly raining
& I found it of some interest.

1

"I didn't want to pass
for white anymore,
                    if you know
what I'm saying.
                    It felt important
to make it known
                    that I'm a Jew."

2

"You're your own train, you got
your own track
                    & you can go anywhere."

3

"Is Jewish music
music made by Jews?

Does it mean music
that connects to the klezmer tradition

or to the Frankfurt School, to
Benjamin or Adorno?

What is it that puts
a Jewish slant
on someone's identity?

That's an ineffable
quality and, perhaps,
to define it
is to destroy it."

Joel Lewis

He wears tzitzes to remind himself
to remain a good person

There's a bit of the Maccabee in him.
  & there's also a bit of the unadulterated jerk.

    The table is filled with many objects.
Our community brightens sundown. Two brachas
over three candles. What is there .
to know? Beneath the sign that symbolizes
signs, a man goes about his waiting
with Tam Tam crackers and cold schav
as companions. Upstairs, the lesbian couple reads
Heather Has Two Mommies to their new-born.
A snow storm punks out over Pittsburgh.
A progressive accordion sextet upsets normalcy.
I'm trying to get up early
for my share of the light but
this, too, fails to work.

While watching the spectacle
of money growing greater
than money itself,
things just keep getting
clearer: the energy
of the Western World
is wasted on the enormous
but absolutely minor
characters that inhabit
the magazine racks.

Talmud: *"A Person is always liable
        for his actions, whether awake
        or asleep."*

The dream heat
is looking for me, I've killed
Nazis and Tartars in slumberland. Tug
at my imaginary tzitzes to remind myself
to be a good person.

                Back at the coffee bar called Diaspora Joe.
                Outside: people's hands seem made of water.
                Inside: Friends and conviviality.

                No end to things built of human talk.

Joel Lewis

"You feel oppressed by your
Judaism only as long
as you do not take pride
in it." So see the earth and
see the people on this earth
and see them all going on with
the business of work, sex, love, dreaming,
hate and growth. Accept the "volitional
affirmation of the obligatory."

Now, you just might think
that the sun is saying,
"Come dance with me," but it isn't.
And you might not like catfish,
but you'll never be sure
if that catfish likes **you** or not.

Poetry after Auschwitz? Sure, why not?! Bygones
will not be bygones, after all.

Rabbi Tarphon: "Yours is not to complete
the work, but neither are you
free to abstain from it."

Beyond Dripping Shabbas Candles

In 1936, Jacob Glatshteyn, arguably one of the greatest of Yiddish language poets, journeyed from the USA to his native Poland to visit his dying mother. Glatshteyn was a member of the *In Zikh* literary movement, the closest Yiddish literature gets to a Modernist stance. The *In Zikh* poets translated Ezra Pound and T. S. Eliot into Yiddish and attempted to give Yiddish a viable place in the European literary continuum. Glatshteyn, for his part, was the first Yiddish poet to publish a book in free verse. In the mid-1930's, he embarked upon a series of Joycean language experiments. The title of one poem. "If Joyce Wrote in Yiddish," seems to sum up the nature of this project.

Upon his arrival in Poland, Glatshteyn was stunned by the state in which he found European Jewry. The world Depression had left the entire community in dire poverty. In addition, the mass emigration that began in the 1880's and ended in the 1920's had simultaneously drained the community of both its upwardly mobile and its less religious families. The result was that Polish Jewry was both deeply religious and deeply fatalistic. The Pidulski regime had made its own contribution to the situation by enacting a series of anti-Semitic legislations that further impoverished the community. Additionally — anticipating the Nazis by a few years — the Polish government had decreed that all Jews had to wear a yellow star armband when in public.

Glatshteyn returned to the US with a premonition of the great catastrophe that was awaiting the European Jewish community. He broke away from his experimentalist aesthetics with the poem, "Goodnight World":

> Good night, wide world,
> great, stinking world.
> Not you but I slam the gate.
> With the long gabardine,
> with the yellow patch — burning —
> with proud stride
> I decide —:
> I am going back to the ghetto.
> Wipe out, stamp out all traces of apostasy.
> I wallow in your filth.
> Blessed, blessed, blessed,
> hunchbacked Jewish life.
> Go to hell, with your polluted cultures, world.
> Though all is ravaged,
> I am dust of your dust,
> sad Jewish life. [Excerpt]

The poem caused a sensation in the Yiddish press upon its initial publication in 1938. From that poem, until his death in 1972, Glatshteyn becomes the great national poet of Yiddish. Consciously, he addresses his poetry to both the remnants of Yiddishkeit and to the great, vast and dead potential readership killed in the *Churban* (the Yiddish equivalent of the term *Holocaust*).

Glatshteyn's transformation from a Joycean experimentalist to an elegiast for *Yiddishkeit* was not a simple one, nor did it have the immediacy of a *fait accompli*. He never abandoned his experimentalist leanings, and he never lapsed into the easy sentimentalism and nostalgia for shtetl life. His stance, in most of his later poems, was that of dual exile. His was a doubled *Galut* (Yiddish for *Diaspora*); he spent his days writing both poems and a vast amount of journalism in a language, and about a culture, that fewer and fewer American Jews cared about. Around the time of the publication of his 1961 volume, *The Joy of the Yiddish Word*, comedians like Alan King and fauxfolk singer Allen Sherman were suggesting that Jewish culture was mostly shtick and of little use to a sterile American Jewish world more focused on Israel than on community concerns. Was Glatshteyn perhaps watching Mickey Katz or Myron Cohen when he wrote these lines: "The television-pane reflected my every word / With a blow of laughter."

The death of Yiddish as a literary language (it is assured a continuance, however, as the lingua franca of the very religious *Chassidic* and *Haredi* communities) ends the possibility of Jewish poets directly addressing an exclusively Jewish audience. Hebrew (despite its obvious claim on Kol Yisrael & its status as the language that tradition holds that God speaks in) is a national language, and so it is spoken by the many non-Jews who live in Israel. Yiddish was a language without a homeland, with the lone exception of the small, unsuccessful attempt by Stalin to establish the Birobadan Yiddish ooblast deep in Siberia. Despite its low status among Zionists, who considered it a constant reminder of the *Galut* mindset, and even among its speakers, who often referred to it as *Jhargon*, it generated a remarkable body of work that speaks directly to the eastern European Jewish sensibility.

How does one "think in Jewish" writing *in* the language of the galut? I have no choice, having little but a small vocabulary and no grammar in either Yiddish or Hebrew. Happily, the post-Olsonic writing scene allows for the immigrant-derived English of myself and others outside the nativist circuit.

I've never felt comfortable with much of American-Jewish poetry. So much depends, in these poems, on the dripping shabbas candles, beside the twisted challah, next to the kiddish cup. No more childhood pieties! Poets who think they are conveying part of their culture in this manner are only telling the audience that for them Judaism is just a childish thing they pull out of their memory junk drawer for occasional display. Ironically, some of the greatest recent poetry that represents the attempt to think in Jewish are by two European writers — Edmond Jabès and

Paul Celan. In addition, few American-Jewish poets have found use for the possibilities suggested by these magnincent writers. A major exception is the wonderful David Meltzer, whose important body of work seems neglected these days. His poetry has been seed-source for those of us who have struggled to create a Jewish-centered poetry that goes beyond the anecdotal, memory-based constructs that fill up too many anthologies.

I write *Nervous Fabric* out of deep concern for Jewish continuity in the American galut. I am troubled by a lack of Jewish literacy in the community. As a Yeshiva student, I used to receive daleds (D's) with red circles about them on my report card — with my rebbes checking: "is doing to the best of his ability." Now, I find myself a local source for Jewish info — which alarms my Yeshiva bocher self. Will we become the new Marranos — a hodgepodge culture of mixed rites and half-remembered rituals? While there seems to be an enormous reawakening about things Jewish (such as the popularity of klezmer music and Kabbala), this renewal also has the quality of an amusement park in its last season before the developers rip it down. Or is all this *kvetching* part of the process? As the philosopher Emanuel Levinas notes: "The very fact of questioning one's Jewish identity means it is already lost. But by the very same token, it is precisely through this kind of cross-examination that one still hangs onto it. Between *already* and *still* Western Judaism walks a tightrope."[*]

---

[*]I do not intend to slight Ladino, the lingua franca of the Sephardic community. Ladino, another stateless language that also offered its speakers an opportunity to "think in Jewish," boasts a broad range of literature and songs. The fact that I do not discuss this rich language reflects the gaps in my education and the limits of the normative Ashkenazic world-view.

Designed by
Samuel Retsov

Text: 10 pt Times
Titles: 13 pt Avant Garde Gothic

acid-free paper

Printed by
McNaughton & Gunn